# EXILE ME

# Exile Me
# تبعیدم کنید

Seyed Morteza
Hamidzadeh

Exile Me Copyright © 2015 by Seyed Morteza Hamidzadeh.

All rights reserved. Printed in the United States of America. No part of this book may be used or reproduced in any manner whatsoever without written permission except in the case of brief quotations em- bodied in critical articles or reviews.

This book is a work of fiction. Names, characters, businesses, organizations, places, events and incidents either are the product of the author's imagination or are used fictitiously. Any resemblance to actual persons, living or dead, events, or locales is entirely coincidental.

For information contact; address www.maudlinhouse.net

Book and Cover design by Maudlin House

ISBN: 978-0-9966595-0-5

First Edition: August 2015

10 9 8 7 6 5 4 3 2 1

Dedicated to my dear father and mother. To my friends, Alfred Corn, Mallory Smart and Jalal Tofighi.

This book is for the martyrs of my country.

## Introduction by editor Mallory Smart

*"My dear friends, I must go to the military camp in Yazd city. We must train in guns & defense against our enemies & extremists...Best wishes for you, Iran is my country with great soldiers ...Peace is always in my heart..."* – Seyed Morteza Hamidzadeh

I know it sounds cliché, and overwrought, but to better prepare you for the poetic journey for which you are about to embark, it is imperative to stress that Seyed Morteza Hamidzadeh was born to be a soldier. Not a soldier of hate or war mind you, but a soldier of the heart. He is the "soldier poet laureate" of our time.

I first came into contact with Seyed after publishing some of his work in Maudlin House's "War & Peace" issue and we immediately hit it off. It was through these initial contacts that I began to see the image of an exotic far-flung poet dissipate, and the image of someone just like me, come clear. Hamidzadeh was born, raised, and lives in a world completely different than the one we know. But he is no different than any of us. Yes, he must face death, insecurity, and disorder on a daily basis, but that doesn't make him any less human or real than the rest of us. Yet everyday the media demonizes and dehumanizes him and his country: painting caricatures of evil and supervillians.

It is time that we dispelled the antiquated distortion of the Iranian screaming "death to America" in the streets, and pay witness to a Persian poet who spends his days training and toiling to fight the same extremists that we do. He studies literature, music, loves sports and America, yet he faces repudiation from the people he loves. In the mere year that I have known him, I have heard of at least three of his young friends dying in the violence that he must face every day. Yet he still lives his life to the fullest. And yes, he also knows people who were killed by ISIS, and he hates them the same as we do. It is time that we let the Iranian culture speak for itself and not let it become saturated by our own media's paranoia and ratings obsessed ego. Hollywood films like Argo and Not Without My Daughter should no longer shape our feelings about an entire nation for they only serve as soundboards of our own fears and micro-aggressions.

At the center of the so-called "Axis Of Evil" lie stories of life and love more compelling than any western rhetoric that we have strained to swallow. In publishing these poems, we hope to help build bridges of understanding and begin a dialogue between the western reader and Iran. Not just in presenting fresh and insightful poetry, but also in reminding others that we have much more in common with this culture than many would consider.

'Exile Me' is a collection of 34 poems presented in both English and Farsi (bridges). These poems act as a living conscience of the times with verse about ISIS, occupying soldiers, and the emotions of wartime. I present them to you with the greatest awe and respect, and urge you, the reader, to digest them with the same awe. We are standing at a unique time in history where we can continue to make the same mistakes as those who came before us, or move forward and find a mutual peace and love between our two peoples.

In the end it will be our understanding, not our anger that will bring us peace.

So I urge you to read Seyed's word with that in mind. This is only the beginning. Seyed Morteza Hamidzadeh is a poet who will just keep on writing.

# Exile Me

Seyed Morteza Hamidzadeh

*Forest of the mind, You will protect this desert war...*

Designed by Seyed Javad Saberi

## CONTENTS

editor's note..................................................................10
passage of time..............................................................18
a girl and the war..........................................................23
step by step...................................................................29
forgotten........................................................................34
excommunication..........................................................39
aggressiveness of century..............................................44
a girl lost in time...........................................................50
empty.............................................................................55
downfall is near.............................................................61
the heart and the hammer..............................................66
holy devils.....................................................................72
blood crime pieces........................................................77
white, but dark..............................................................82
terror's decay.................................................................87
foolish eyes...................................................................92
desecrated youth............................................................97
a crack in time.............................................................102
song of refuge.............................................................107
divine inhumanity ......................................................112
scamps of war.............................................................117
escape..........................................................................122
souls of the country....................................................127
love drop down...........................................................133
the silent uproar..........................................................139
storms of famine.........................................................145
captive.........................................................................151
you, to me...................................................................157
generation killers........................................................162
blood offerings...........................................................167
life measured..............................................................173
consumed impartial....................................................179
we might be dead.......................................................184
call of the disrupt.......................................................189
not duplicated, transcended.......................................194
about the author.........................................................199

Seyed Morteza Hamidzadeh

## Exile Me

# Seyed Morteza Hamidzadeh

# Passage Of Time

گذر زمان

## Seyed Morteza Hamidzadeh

Sand. Soil. A mountain.

Storm threatening

& The shepherd doesn't have his dog.

خاک ها بر کوه می سایند

هوایی طوفان زده

و چوپانی بدون سگ .

Seyed Morteza Hamidzadeh

# Exile Me

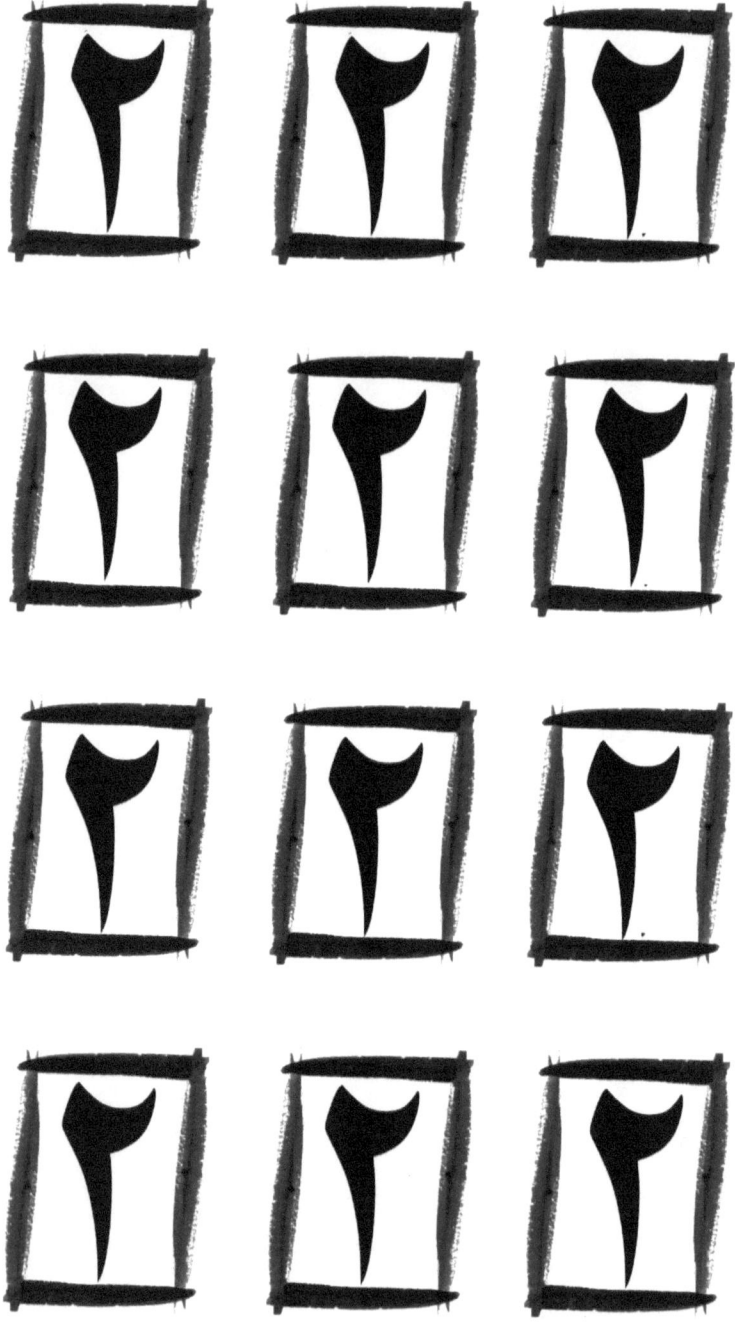

Seyed Morteza Hamidzadeh

# A Girl & The War

دختر و جنگ

## Exile Me

My entire being
Is a battleground, in which
The Leper Writers, make their interpretation in the
encyclopedia of tumbledown homes.

The newly returned wounded of war,
Remove bandages from their bullet-stricken feet.

Boots after boots are being taken off,
announcing their arrivals to families,
so that the long period of anticipation is ended!

Wind is blowing,
and the child,
goes to the father's bedside.

Wind is blowing,
Mother holds the child in her bosom.

Wind is blowing,
but the girl, still young,
is the spectator of a weary horde of soldiers,
carrying the frigidity of her husband's corpse,
through the rushing crowd.

وجودم ،

میدان جنگی است

که نویسندگان جذامی

در دایره المعارف خانه های ویران شده

تفسیر کردند

و زخمیان تازه از جنگ برگشته

پانسمان پاهای تیرخورده شان را

باز می کنند.

و چکمه

چکمه

که از پا در می آمد

تا ورود خود را به خانواده هایشان

اعلام کنند

زمان انتظار به پایان می رسد.

باد می وزد و

کودک

به بالین پدرش می رود

## Exile Me

باد می وزد و

مادر

فرزندش را در آغوش می گیرد

باد می وزد، اما

دختر جوان

نظاره گر فوج سربازان خسته ایست

که زمهریر پیکر شوهرش را

لابه لای هجوم مردم

می بیند.

Seyed Morteza Hamidzadeh

# Exile Me

Seyed Morteza Hamidzadeh

# Step by Step

قدم به قدم

## Exile Me

Step by step,

Nested corridors

Premature images

Which are more mysterious than wisdom

Are passing from my closed eyes

In the bed of the gypsies lane market

Gathering of wolf and ewe tribes are going on

Smell of contract and treaty,

Ever lasting peace and expanse of land,

Which, this dirty bloods flowing in the vessels without vessel liberty

Will make posterity flow

My wife,

Sings lullabies to our child

Tomorrow there will be war.

## Seyed Morteza Hamidzadeh

قدم به قدم،

راهروهای تو در تو

تصاویر نابهنگام

که مرموزانه تر از عقل اند

عبور میکنند

از چشمان بسته ام

در بستر کولیان کوچه و بازار

گردهمایی قبایل گرگ و میش

در پیش است

بوی قرارداد و عهدنامه،

صلح نامیرا و وسعت سرزمین

که آیندگان را

این چرکین خونهای جاری

در رگ های بی رگ آزادی

به جریان می اندازد.

زن،

برای فرزندمان لالایی بخوان

فردا روز جنگ است.

# Exile Me

# Seyed Morteza Hamidzadeh

# Forgotten

فراموش شده

O, witnesses of the night
Exile me
To the most distant point of the universe
In the complex area of the vacuum
Moment by moment
I think about my enjoyment
That night
the voice of the calligrapher's pen was heard
And I feigned sleep
I became tired
Time
is my place to act
I have acknowledged my faith
I shall go to the cemetery
To dig a grave for myself
but
The weather is cold
It's snowing
And umbrellas
Have put my burial ceremony off.

# Exile Me

ای شاهدان شب

تبعیدم کنید

به دوردست ترین نقطه کائنات

آن بی کرانه های افتاده در خلا

لحظه ای تا لحظه ای

به لذت هایم فکر میکنم

شبی که

ندای قلم خطاط را شنیدم

و خود را به خواب زدم

دیگر خسته شدم

زمان،

عرصه عمل من است

ایمان آورده ام

به گورستان میروم

تا قبری برای خود بکنم

اما، هوا سرد است

برف می آید

و چترها

مراسم تدفین مرا عقب انداخته اند.

# Exile Me

Seyed Morteza Hamidzadeh

# Excommunication

تكفير

## Exile Me

Everyone would have abandoned you,
but an executed Angel in your heart,
who sent out the resurrection of her brain
to the slaughtering field of the Trumpeters,
and the duel-declaration of two eyes,
with the edge of your breathing
which challenged the world of your ears.

Oh, philosophical nightmares of mine!
My lips lack the ability to move.

I wish for setting myself ablaze,
as do the meteors entering the atmosphere.

O' religions of the world,
enunciate the decree of my excommunication
and allow the shepherds to breathe with ease.

همه،

تو را تنها می گذارند

جز فرشته ای اعدام شده

در قلبت

که رستاخیز مغزش را،

به قتلگاه شیپورزنان فرستاد

و آگهی دوئل دو چشم

با مرز نفس کشیدنت،

جهان گوش ات را

به چالش انداخت


آه

کابوس های فلسفی من

لبانم توان حرکت ندارند

می خواهم

بسوزانم خود را

همچون شهاب های رسیده به جو


ادیان الهی،

حکم تکفیر مرا

## Exile Me

صادر کنید

بگذارید چوپانان

نفس راحتی بکشند.

# Seyed Morteza Hamidzadeh

# Aggressiveness of Century

تجاوزگران قرن

These figures fallen

In the swamp of the infertile females

Are the men

In the land of the wine and alcohol

Who throw their sheets

On the ground

And think of sleeping with the beasts

Oh

For crave-like brains filled with coal

There is no mirror

To servant themselves.

Fields of sunflowers

Are the breaks

At the time of Motion while moving

Dawn is near

Yeah

Dawn of Black coated!!


Shadows will not be waiting anymore

They will be faded

And you will be swallowed inside of them.

این چهره های افتاده

در باتلاق زنان نازا

مردانی اند

در سرزمین شراب و الکل

که ورق هایشان را

بر زمین می اندازند

و به هم بستری با چهارپایان فکر میکنند

آه

زغال مغزان غارصفت

آینه ای نیست

خود را خادم کند به خود

مزارع گلهای آفتابگردان

توقفی ست از حرکت در حرکت

طلوع، نزدیک است

آری

طلوع سیاه جامگان

سایه ها بیش از این در انتظار نخواهند ماند

آنان محو میشوند

و تو را در خود خواهند بلعید.

# Exile Me

# Seyed Morteza Hamidzadeh

# A Girl Lost in Time

دختر زمانهای از دست رفته

Sound of Azan
And girl,
Standing by the street
With her foot leaning against the wall
Thoughtful
Counts her childhood's dolls
Her mind sways
Amid the vacuum of gentle touch
And some who go to the mosque.
The girl
Standing by the street
A few men get close, prating
To show her a shelter
In return for a moment of vomiting touch
Sound of Azan, two times ((there is no god but Allah))
And the wall,
That is not her support anymore.

## Exile Me

صدای اذان و

دختر،

کنار خیابان ایستاده

با پایی که بر دیوار تکیه داده است

در خود فرو رفته و

عروسک های کودکی اش را می شمارد

و ذهنی که می چرخد

میان خلاء نوازش

و عده ای که به مسجد می روند.


دختر، کنار خیابان ایستاده

چند مرد با یاوه گویی نزدیک می شوند

و پناهگاهی را نشان می دهند

به لحظه ای نوازش تهوع آور


صدای اذان،

دو بار (( لا اله الا الله ))

و دیواری که دیگر

تکیه گاه دختر نیست.

# Seyed Morteza Hamidzadeh

# Exile Me

Seyed Morteza Hamidzadeh

# Empty

تهی

## Exile Me

The sun sets, small pools
of water stop vaporizing
and once again, jackals
ever-ready predators pounce
on the vulnerable nests
of birds. Thus rises a call
from the West,
and another cry
from the East.

Night falls on the blacksmith
whose Kaviyani pennant is covered
with dust. And darkness
like napery, or the dead-
eating explorers.

Don't abandon me!
The Shrine I have chosen
has been bewitched
by those who forge
words and statues.

## Seyed Morteza Hamidzadeh

خورشید،

بی پروا غروب می کند

و حوضچه های آب

از تبخیر باز می ایستند


و دوباره شغالان،

این نابهنجاران آماده به شبیخون،

بر لانه های بی پناه مرغان

حمله ور می شوند


آواز از مغرب و فریاد از مشرق

آغاز می شود


شب به آهنگری خواهد شد

که درفش کاویانش را

خاک گرفته است

و سیاهی سفره ای ماند

به سان مرده خواران کاشف


رهایم مکنید

در این سرزمین نامقدس

معبدی که برگزیدم

مسحور جاعلان هر لفظ و مقامی شده است.

Seyed Morteza Hamidzadeh

# Exile Me

Seyed Morteza Hamidzadeh

# Downfall is Near

سقوط نزدیک است

## Exile Me

Open the mad houses
The wise men have grown mad
Lines of rotten meats!

O' chiggers
Assail
Darkness has reached
Withhold the water to be reached
Just the ocean is saline

And will never become desalinated
Cut the vulture's wings
With boundless tongues
For they would not prowl
In the dead's sky.

The graves' voices
Are exposed to the sun

Yea
O' gods of wane dormitory
Downfall is about to occur.

## Seyed Morteza Hamidzadeh

دیوانه خانه ها را باز کنید

عاقلان، بی عقل شده اند

صفوف گوشت های گندیده

ساس ها

حمله کنید

تاریکی رسیده است

مگذارید آبی برسد

تنها ،

اقیانوس شور است

که شیرین نمی شود

با زبان های بی مرز

قطع کنید

بال های لاشخوران را

تا پرسه نزنند

بر آسمان مردگان

ندای گورها رو به قبله است

آری

خدایگان خوابگاه خیزش

سقوط، نزدیک است.

# Exile Me

# The Heart & The Hammer

قلب و چکش

# Seyed Morteza Hamidzadeh

In the Forum of blacksmiths
Steel and iron are melted.
Someone from one side
Shouting
Our wages have been set on fire
Our wages've been overwhelmed by the furnace controversy
By the opiated melts,
The seconds of present trend to the past
Someone with tooth-pick in his mouth
With a pressed fist
Which carries the time
Said: ((shut up))
This time louder than before,
Wage, wage
Others off, deeply look at him.
One, two, three, four ...
S Counting brutality look
Six o'clock,
One stare,
What did you want?
Oh! Wage!
Laughter, laughter
And starting to whine
Which did not struck any ears.
Blood, flowing blood
Decorated the table
And the last carcasses
Were thinking of freedom
Now the heaven
has been provided for buzzards.

## Exile Me

در سرسرای تالار چکش به دستان
فولاد و آهن ذوب میشود.
کسی از سویی
فریاد برمی آورد
دست مزدمان را به زیر آتش برده اند
به زیر جنجال کوره ،
به زیر مذابهای افیون شده ،
ثانیه های حال، به گذشته میروند
فردی خلال به دهان
با فشرده دستی که
زمان را حمل میکند، گفت: (( خفه شو ))
این بار بلندتر از قبل ،
دست مزد ، دست مزد
دیگرانِ خاموش، غرق در او مینگرند.
یک ، دو ، سه چهار ...
شمارش نگاه حیوانیت
ساعت شش ،
تک نگاهی خیره ،
خواسته ات چه بود ؟
آها ! دست مزد!
قهقهه ، قهقهه
و شروع ناله ای که هیچ گوشی را نمی لرزاند.

## Seyed Morteza Hamidzadeh

خون ، خون روان

بر میزش نقش بسته است

و آخرین لاشه ها

به آزادی فکر کردند.

کنون برای لاشخوران، آسمانی فراهم شده است.

Exile Me

# Holy Devils

شياطين قديس

## Seyed Morteza Hamidzadeh

Holy devils,
Are guardians of prostitutes alleys
In this way
The residents of anger and wrath
Are goddess that their wildly neighbors originated of ape and thirst
To spread out the ash of their with no baptism sin
On the particular without armour

Look at,
The certain day
Ocean will bring it octopus from depth to the surface

That day
Will have been regret day of sunny ghostliness.

## Exile Me

شیاطین قدیس،

نگهبانان کوچه های روسپیانند

اینسان

ساکنان قهر و غضب

خدایانی اند

که همسایگان وحشی نشان

از تبار بوزینه و عطش اند

تا خاکستر گناه بی تعمیدشان را

بر ذرات بی زره

پخش کنند.

نگاه کنید

به روز معین

اقیانوس

اختاپوس هایش را

از ژرف به سطح می آورد

آن روز

روز حسرتِ شبح وارگان خورشیدی

خواهد بود.

Seyed Morteza Hamidzadeh

# Exile Me

Seyed Morteza Hamidzadeh

# Blood Crime Pieces

خون پاره های جنایت

## Exile Me

Wine glasses

on the officer's desk

the imprinted a plan

twisted with

shapes of circles and angles

smoke up to the ceiling

the chairs keeping the ranks clothes hang

on skin of the floor

open the windows of commands room

dead bodies of soldiers

have fallen in a corner

why don't you respect the real victors?

Cool down,

Only the wings of some flies

Wipe away the dust

Of your bodies.

جام های شراب

روی میز افسران

نقشه ای نقش بسته

پیچیده شده

با دوایر و زاویه ها

دودهای رفته تا سقف

صندلیهایی که لباسهای درجه داران را

نگه میدارد بر پوستین کف

پنجره های اتاق فرماندهی را باز کنید

جنازه های سربازان

به گوشه ای افتاده اند

چرا به فاتحان واقعی احترام نمی گذارید؟

آرام گیرید،

تنها

بالهای چند مگس

گرد و غبار را

از پیکرهایتان میزداید

# Exile Me

# White, but dark

سفید، اما سیاه

Mausoleum of jackals
Is leprous
Jackals' mouths are full of blood
The meats have become rotten in their stomachs

Plateau
Has not seen a herd in itself for a while

Dogs
Have become intoxicated

On the summits of wickedness
And have left the custody
to the wolves.

## Exile Me

جذامی ست

مقبره شغالان

دهانی پر از خون

گوشتهایی که در معده هایشان فاسد شده

دشت

چند وقتی ست گله ای در خود ندیده

سگان

در قله های شقاوت

مست شده اند

و نگاهبانی را

به گرگ ها سپرده اند.

Seyed Morteza Hamidzadeh

# Exile Me

Seyed Morteza Hamidzadeh

# Terror's Decay

دهه ترور

# Exile Me

The grave voice announcing your martyrdom

From Time's momentariness till Eternity -

The bursting chatter of birds ensues

Till the beauty of sunset -

We kissed goodbye

Thrones that gave rise to qibla.

And got killed

The blowing up of minds

And bleeding of stomachs

out of fear

of getting decayed pervades

The aura of emphasis

Tattered with holes -

A cracking bullet inside decades

And Fragrance

On the other side - of your head -

Shhh..

Someone is pointing a gun at your head

## Seyed Morteza Hamidzadeh

آواز حلق‌آویز شهیدشدن‌ات

از زمان به پایان و

انفجار چهچهه‌ی پرندگانی

تا به زیبندگی غروب رسیدن

ما بوسیدیم و خواباندیم

تخت‌هایی را که قبله رویاندند.

ما شهید شدیم

ضربه‌ای بر مغز و خونریزی معده از ترس فاسد شدن

بوی فهماندن ،

سوراخ‌سوراخ می‌شود

گلویی ترک‌خورده در قرن

بویی است ،

از آن‌طرف کلمات !

هیس ...

کسی بر مغزت

تفنگ دوربین‌دار بسته است .

## Exile Me

# Foolish Eyes

چشمان احمقانه

## Seyed Morteza Hamidzadeh

We remain in the celebration of fools

But you should have said that the eye

Doesn't remain open

Bone burning coldness

Has kept me firm

From the morning of the west

You scream timelessly

From glory shined upon indifferent wisdoms

From losing more than enough

A picture better than astonishment of eyes in

A small camera

Ever since we have known him

He would move higher to the fasting duality

Of me: jagged and irrelevant gatherings

The wetness of the book that wouldn't dry in a hundred years

From the stubborn look of words!!!

## Exile Me

در جشنِ احمق‌ها می‌مانم
مگر می‌گفتی که چشم
باز نمی‌ماند
سردیِ استخوان‌سوز
مرا ثابت نگه‌می‌داشته‌اند
از صبحِ مغربی
بی‌هرزمان زار می‌زنی
از شکوه تابیده بر خردهای لاابالی
از دست‌دادن‌های بیش از حد
عکسی بهتر از خیرگی‌های چشمی در
دوربین عکاسی کوچک ...
از هر زمان که می‌شناختیمش
بالاتر می‌رفته تا ناشتای دوگانگی
منِ ناهموار گردهمایی‌های بی‌ربط و
خیسی کتابی که صدساله خشک می‌شد
از نگاهِ خیره در واژه‌ها !!!

Seyed Morteza Hamidzadeh

## Exile Me

Seyed Morteza Hamidzadeh

# Desecrated Youth

جوانان در معرض بیحرمتی

## Exile Me

For the quivers of your body

A vow up your sleeve

And gunshots of disgrace of the underpass.

I shall stay there and watch that you

Are being called impure,

Woe to the hand on your skin, woe to the moments of coming out of the hearth

Of your visage…

The child looks out of the window,

Inside the car and mother excuses you…

Don't get close to her!

And the creation you glorified

Lousy creation, of sinister mold

And you, the outset of the passersby can

Be summarized in a line,

Modern and postmodern fools

To bloody lowers and scents of lust…

برای لرزش تن‌ات

سوگندی در آستین‌ات

و تیررس رسوایی‌های زیررو.

من آنجا می‌مانم و می‌نگرم که تو را

نجس می‌خوانند ،

مباد دستی بر پوست‌ات، مباد که لحظه‌ای از اجاق بیرون آید

صورت‌ات ...

کودک از پنجره می‌نگرد ،

سوار بر ماشین و مادر معذور می‌داردت ...

به او نزدیک مشو !

و خلقتی که افتخار نمودی

خلقت شپش، کالبد منحوس

و تو می‌توان شروعی از عابران را

در خطی خلاصه کنی ،

دلقک‌های مدرنیته و پست مدرن

به شلوارهای خونی و بوالهوس ...

# Exile Me

# A Crack In Time

شکاف در زمان

Sometimes to the vein,

Sometimes to the council…

A crack in time,

Harsher than frostbite…

Inside someone,

A hundred voices on the body…

You are listening while asleep,

Deaf, killers of spite…

He still believed in power

Blows taken on head

A mind in the blow…

Like a fading reason,

In calculations of universe!

## Exile Me

رگ تا گاه ،
رگ به شورا ...
ترک تو گاه ،
خشن‌تر از سرمازدگان ...
درون کسی ،
صد صدا بر تن ...
تویی بر خفتن گوش ،
ناشنوایان بُغض‌کُشان ...
هنوز باور توان کرد
ضربه‌های خورده بر سر
مغزی است در ضربه ...
همچنان عقلی زایل ،
در محاسبات کائنات !

Seyed Morteza Hamidzadeh

# Exile Me

Seyed Morteza Hamidzadeh

# Song of Refuge

نغمه پناهندگی

## Exile Me

A man, weathered

On the throat inside…

The man looks at the same land

With a warm hand…

A woman became the summary of everything

Showing affection and kissing…

The woman showed the refuge of the dolls

Day and night…

And the boy,

Went to pursue the anecdotes from fables

Naked and unarmed…

Afterwards as they invaded the door,

The girls paved the way

So that no one,

Would swear in the name of their leaders!

مردی، زمان کوبید

بر حلق خود اندر ...

مردی، همان سرزمین را نگریست

با دستی گرم ...

زنی، خلاصه شد در همه چیز

مهر ورزیدن و بوسیدن ...

زنی، پناه عروسک‌ها را نشان داد

روزی و شبی ...

و پسر ،

به دنبال حکایت‌هایی از افسانه‌ها رفت

عُریان و بی‌سلاح ...

آنگاه که بر در تاختند ،

دخترانی، راه را هموار کردند

که هیچ‌کسی ،

به رهبرانشان سوگند نمی‌خورد !

# Exile Me

# Divine Inhumanity

نامردمان قديس

## Seyed Morteza Hamidzadeh

Tonight,

All neighbors have been invited

Blue draught is put upon the table and

People over the casket!!!

Someone,

Plays love and gets

Multiple executions of their mouths…

Hands in prayer,

are buzzing and the ancestress of city,

Raises a family of the saint!!!

Grandchildren away from the city

And hideous cries of spectators…

Me: tired in the abandonment of time

I go on the scene

Scene of blood gushing and

Being next to each other…

## Exile Me

امشب ،

تمام همسایه‌ها دعوت شده‌اند

جرعه آبی بر میز و

نفراتِ بر تابوت !!!

کسی ،

عشق‌بازی می‌کند و می‌گیرد

تعدد اعدام دهان‌هایشان ...

کفِ دست‌ها در قنوت ،

وزوز می‌کند و مادربزرگ شهر ،

خاندانِ پیر می‌آفریند !!!

نوه‌هایی به دور از شهر

و گریه‌های کریهِ تماشاگران ...

منِ خسته در هرزه‌گاهِ زمان

به روی صحنه می‌روم

صحنه‌ی خون‌فشانی و

بودنِ در کناره‌ها ...

Seyed Morteza Hamidzadeh

# Exile Me

Seyed Morteza Hamidzadeh

# Scamps Of War

لمس جنگ

## Exile Me

On you till unlikely of you,

Closed the eyes!

What is this,

Interpretation of my brothers' stones?

Dormant secrets so the coldness of hand

Blood killer…

Nor should the woman shout voices from childhood

Tired of incantations and whispers

In the inscription of description in the described.

Stop… Stop!!!

Loaded with a bomb in your mouth and back and hands.

Stop… Stop!!!

بر تو تا بعیدِ بودنِ از تو ،
چشم روی هم گذاشت !
این چیست ،
تعبیر سنگ‌های برادرانم ؟
رازهای خفته تا سردیِ دستی
خون‌کُش ...
نه زنی می‌بایدش از کودکی در حنجره ،
خسته از ورد و زمزمه
در ثبتِ صفت اندر موصوف‌ها .
ایست ... ایست !!!
پر از بمبی در دهان و کمر و دستانات .
ایست ... ایست !!!

# Exile Me

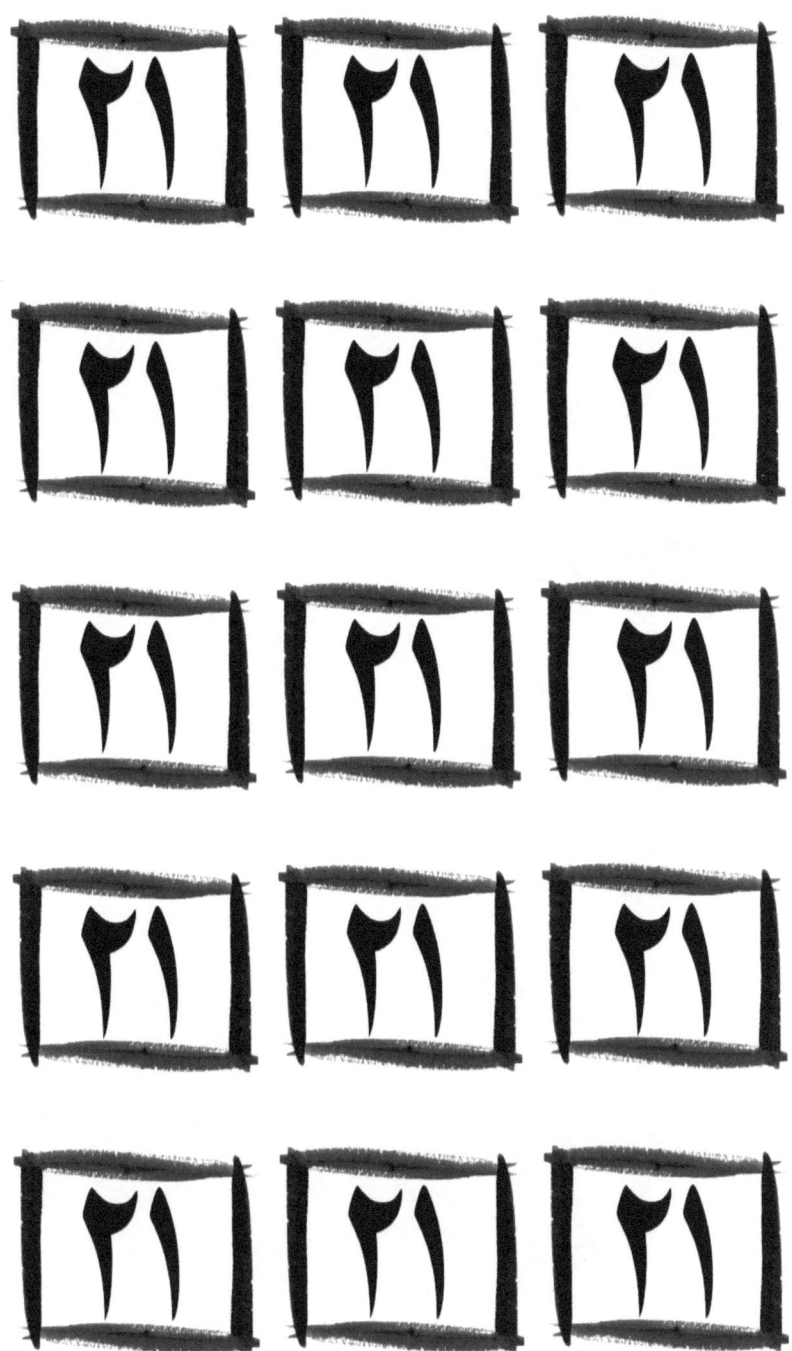

Exile Me

# Escape

فرار

## Seyed Morteza Hamidzadeh

You prefer fleeing to staying

When your generation gets killed

You laugh insanely and in isolation

Laugh many times over…

The debris of migrants are close to you

And only,

With your rucksack on your back, you laugh

And you don't know

What way they will divert their path to?

Newborn in the lap of a woman,

A child handed down from a start till an end

And you laugh without regard

For you get volleyed from the height to the ground…

All your forces

Get exhausted from you laughing incessantly

A few lament and

Burn their hearts over their dead

And you kiss the foreheads of their dead

And often

Sacrifice your smile for them…

## Exile Me

فرار را به ماندن ترجیح می دهی

وقتی نسل ات کشته می شود

می خندی و در انزوا

بارها می خندی ...

آوار مهاجران به تو نزدیک اند

و تنها،

با کوله پشتی ات به پشت، می خندی

و نمی دانی

اینان به کدامین جهت، تغییر مسیر می دهند؟

نوزادی در آغوش زنی،

کودکی دست به دست شده از آغازی به پایانی

و تو بی محابا می خندی

چنانکه از ارتفاعی شلیک میشوی به پایین ...

تمام قوای ات

به خنده های پی در پی ختم می شود

عده ای ضجه می زنند و

بر مرده هاشان دل می سوزانند

و تو بر پیشانی مردگانشان بوسه می زنی

و بارها

لبخندت را نثارشان می‌کنی ...

Seyed Morteza Hamidzadeh

# Exile Me

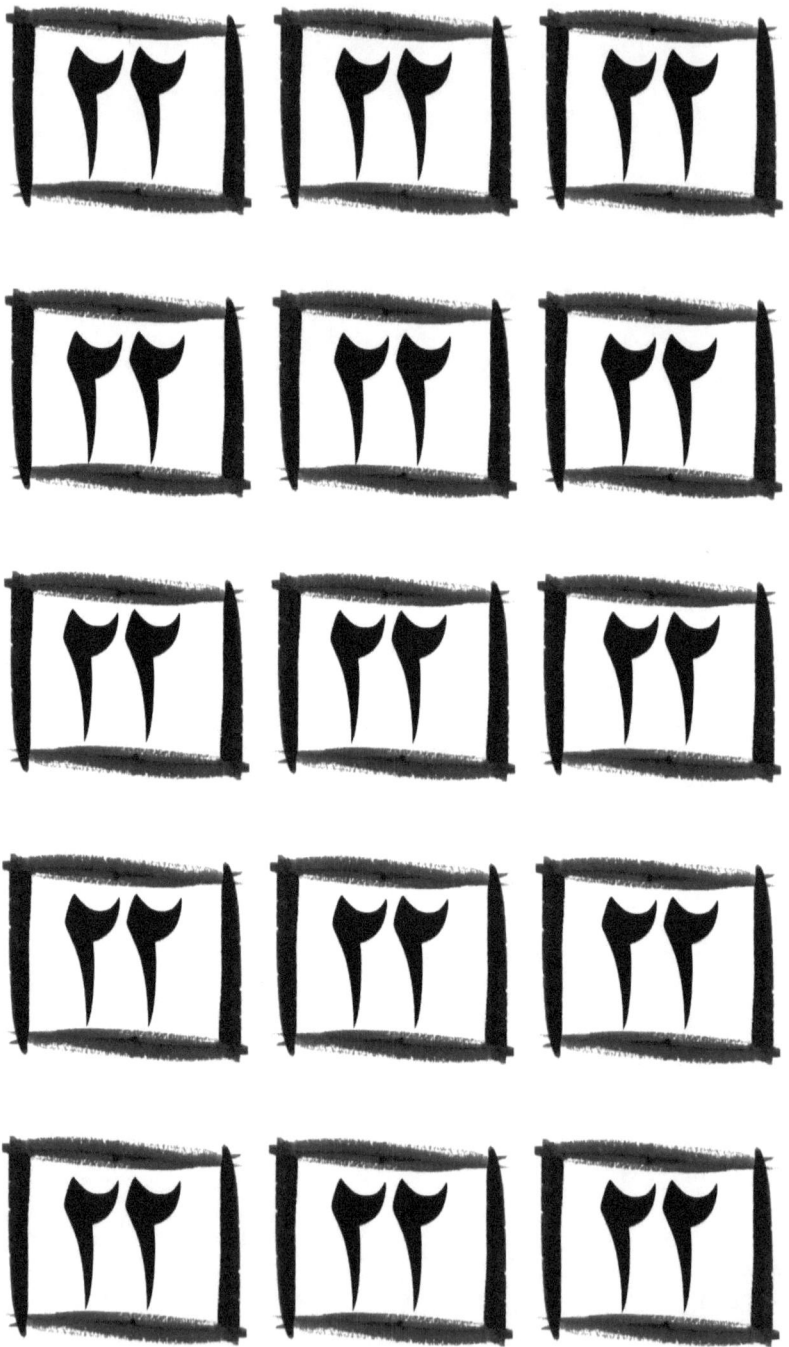

Seyed Morteza Hamidzadeh

# Souls of the Country

ارواح وطنی

## Exile Me

Girl fitted in a baggage

As the Aerial frontier gets occupied

Few well armed cross the public sphere and

Someone passes with a baggage -

Boy,

Slowly moves close, far

From ground…

In the coach, a child, his lips open

He opens them to the aggression of passersby

And they fret in a moment and

A woman stripped

Opens the vibes of that side of border

And in a second,

Takes the stock on her head

Blood-flow,

Slowly like the melting of candle

Goes to the gut of waters

## Seyed Morteza Hamidzadeh

And the plasma,

Drives the cells of city to bed...!

And radio changes its course

To a different frequency.

## EXILE ME

دخترِ جاشده در چمدان

مرزِ هوایی اِشغال می‌شود

چند زره‌پوش از حریم عمومی عبور می‌کنند و

کسی با چمدان می‌گذرد

پسر،

آهسته نزدیک‌دور می‌رود

از میدان ...

در کالسکه، کودک لبانش را بازِ باز

به هجمه عابران باز می‌کند

و در ثانیه‌ای خورده می‌شوند و

زنی عریان‌شده،

فرکانس آنسوی مرزها را می‌گشاید

و در ثانیه‌ای،

قنداقِ تفنگ به سر می‌خورد

خون‌های جاری،

آهسته چون آب شدن شمعی

به بطن آب‌ها می‌رود

و خونابه،

سلولِ شهری را به بستر می‌کِشاند ...!

و رادیو به فرکانسی دیگر

تغییر مسیر می‌دهد.

# Seyed Morteza Hamidzadeh

# Exile Me

Seyed Morteza Hamidzadeh

# Love Falls

سقوط عشق

## Exile Me

You cure my mental illnesses

Separate my head from my body and

He charges at a caravan

The clumped moist veins of nobody

You have handed me over, manacled, in such a way

I can't stand and sleep

Or kiss you.

A child reaches the edge

A border that is red

And in his food packets

He distributes the body parts of people like us

Come and lick

Lick the escalation of the much

Take the game in a lighter vein

Take to frivolity

By the remote seaside

## Seyed Morteza Hamidzadeh

By the extravagant lovers

By the braying of the donkeys…

بیماری‌های روانی‌ام را درمان می‌کنی
سرم را از تن جدا و
کاروانی را به تیر می‌بندد.
خیس رگ‌های توأمان هیچ کسم
چنان مرا دست‌بسته تحویل داده‌اید که
نمی‌توان خوابید و ایستاد
یا تو را بوسید .

کودکی به لب می‌رسد
مرزی که قرمز است
و در بسته‌های غذایی‌اش
تکه‌تکه بدن‌های همنو عمان را توزیع می‌کند
بیا و لیس بزن
لیس بزن از زیادشدن‌های بسیار
بازی را به سخره بگیر و
خودت را به بی‌خیالی بزن
کنار سواحلی دورافتاده
کنار معشوقگان افراط
کنار عرعر خران ...

Seyed Morteza Hamidzadeh

# Exile Me

Seyed Morteza Hamidzadeh

# Silent Uproar (for Omar Al-Fazil)

غوغای سکوت

## Exile Me

Sigh in the mirror incessantly

Your visage

No cupbearer in the mirror

Smell the moment

My pain is astonishedly suspended

Don't think that no girl is destined for you

Or wings of the influenced shall abuse you.


You sister in the frame and you are tired

Whispers... it is a different sound

Neither is it time for adhan nor time to be more patient

You aren't facing the qibla, they wont take you to the qibla


The denial of your childhood days is discovered

As you aged from the separation of walls

## Seyed Morteza Hamidzadeh

Tilted in a moment

Devils have read your testimony

I bear witness that there is no…

Fragrance of the French perfume, toothpaste of your sister

Fragrance of east,

Fragrance of…

## Exile Me

بی وقفه " ها ... " کن در آینه
چهره‌ات
نه می‌نگاری در آینه
بو کن به لحظه‌ای ...
خیره‌آویخته درد من
نه که گمان ببری هیچ دختری نصیبت نخواهد شد
یا ناسزا گویدت بال‌های موجی‌شوندگان.

خواهرت در قاب و تو خسته‌ای
زمزمه ... آه نوای دیگری است
نه گاه اذان است و نه بیش از‌این صبور باش
رو به قبله نیستی، تو را به قبله نمی‌برند.

رد ِ خردسالی‌ات کشف شد
وقتی عمرت گذشت از جدارِ دیوارهای
کج‌شده در لحظه‌ای که
اشهدت را خوانده‌اند عفریتگان
اشهد ان لا ...
بوی عطر فرانسوی، خمیر دندان خواهرت
بوی شرق ،
بوی ...

Seyed Morteza Hamidzadeh

# Exile Me

Seyed Morteza Hamidzadeh

# Storms of Famine
طوفان قحطی

## Exile Me

On the minarets that

No one has seen you

The storm of famines on your black shirt

Suffering is some stranger

Till it reaches you

Successive attacks towards you

Two sleepy bodies…


Futile repetitions, exchanges of statesmanship

Teach haste

A Friday mixed on every…

And Saturday, standstill of breathing on heart

He puts on a red dress and

Everyone gathers at the end of Sunday

Hands wound around the throat

And the usual abstraction

## Seyed Morteza Hamidzadeh

He takes the wild children to the back of the barracks

So that he compels the muezzin to kill

Killings have escalated and afternoon

We go to welcome him

When no one stands,

We make our hearts shields

Winds from it

Have taken us to the roofs of mosques


The standing slave and skin

On his body, a decree…

## Exile Me

بر مناره‌هایی که
هیچ‌کس تو را ندیده است
طوفانِ خشک‌سال‌ها بر پیراهن مشکی‌ات
رنج چند غریبه است
تا به تو رسد
حمله‌های پیاپی به سویت
دو تن‌فرسای خفته ...

بیهوده مکررها به رخ، پاپاپای زمامداری‌هایت
تعجیل می‌آموزند
جمعه‌ای آمیخته به هر ...
و شنبه، ایستِ تنفس به قلب
لباس قرمز بر تن می‌کند و
همگان در یکشنبه پایانی به‌هم می‌رسند
دستِ پیچانده شده به گلو
و انتزاع همیشگی
کودکانِ یاغی را به پشت سنگر می‌برد
تا موذن را وادار به کشتن کنند
کشته‌ها زیاد شده و ظهر
ایستاده به پیشوازش می‌رویم
وقتی کسی نایستد،
ما دل‌هامان را سپر می‌کنیم
بادهایی از همان
ما را به پشتِ‌بام مسجدها بُرده است

بَرده‌ای که ایستاده و پوست
بر تن‌اش حکم بسته ...

Seyed Morteza Hamidzadeh

# Exile Me

Seyed Morteza Hamidzadeh

# Captive

اسیر

## Exile Me

Slapping of children continues

No one is busy with playing

No one is going to pamper you

Your brother passes by the corner and

You are the only sister whose

Lap he needs for comfort…


Before going away from all imaginative fables

Your heartbeats after anything

Mother, father;

And your brother gags mouth with a cloth and

Drinking water without draught, moves away from you

You derive comfort from cement blocks

And air raids

Would take you far-off where…

## Seyed Morteza Hamidzadeh

Remember the powers of pools,

From this side of dizziness

Cage inside cage, he shouts more strongly

Rusted bars of the door

Moisture above its kinds

And night passes the half

City screams more clearly than before!

سیلی بچه‌ها ادامه دارد
کسی به بازی مشغول نیست
کسی تو را نوازش نمی‌کند
برادرت از گوشه‌ای می‌گذرد و
تنها خواهری هستی که
به آغوشت نیازمند است ...


قبل از رفتن به دور از تمام داستان‌های تخیلی
ضربان قلبِ تو را بعد از همه چیز
پدر، مادر ؛
و برادرت پارچه‌ای می پیچاند بر دهان و
بی‌جرعه نوشیدن آبی، از تو دور می‌شود
با بلوکه‌های سیمانی آرام می‌گیری
و بمباران هوایی
می‌پردت به دوردست‌هایی که ...


به یادباش قوای حوض‌ها،
از این سوی دوارها
قفس در قفس محکم‌تر فریاد می‌زند
میله های زنگ زده در
رطوبت بالای گونه‌هایش
و شب از نیمه عبور می‌کند و
شهر بیش از گذشته روشن‌تر فریاد می‌کشد !

Seyed Morteza Hamidzadeh

# Exile Me

Seyed Morteza Hamidzadeh

# You, To Me

تو به من

## Exile Me

We ought to give all artificial breathing

Mouth to mouth

And from a corner you look for me

Undoubtedly you shall see me

Undoubtedly you to me

You have got sky, soil and field

On that side of dispute of body and soul

Yields…

The silence of sleepy glance

He has seen aforetime the completeness that

We have allied for occupation

For your desert degrades several times

Your bones beckoned the thirsty

And a dead body under the sun

Decomposed and its wreckage

Has been distributed for the division of chores!

باید به همگان، تنفسی مصنوعی دهیم
دهان به دهان
و از گوشه‌ای مرا جستجو می‌کنی
بی‌شک مرا خواهی دید
بی‌شک تو را به من
آسمان، خاک و مزرعه‌داری
آن‌سویِ جدالِ روح و تن
ارزانی می‌دارد ...

سَکتِ نگاهِ خفته
پیش‌تر دیده است تمامیتی را که
برای اِشغال پیوستیم
تجزیه می‌شود که بارها صحرایت
تشنه‌ای را به استخوان‌هایت فراخوانده
و جسدی که به زیر آفتاب
پوسیده و لاشه‌هایش
برای تقسیم وظایف، توزیع شده است !

## Exile Me

# Generation Killers

قاتلان نسل

## Seyed Morteza Hamidzadeh

Your heads need to plead so much

That everyone is retrieved from other's coffins

Descendent-less ones mounted on..


There, the guards have seen me

They have to the right a bullet and I must

Touch your hands as quick as possible

I don't feel any comfort and let your hands be

Or at least I shall touch the skewedness of the world

Many selves have become generation-killers

They have circled the miracle

Leave the mouth full of blood

Keep its drops in your cup and flee

The border guard has contracted you…

سرهایتان باید اینقدر
التماست کنند
تا از تابوت دیگران، همه را بازیابند
بی‌نسل‌ها خود سوار بر ...

آنجا مرا نگاهبانان دیده‌اند
حق تیر دارند و باید
دستانت را هر چه سریع‌تر لمس کنم
آرام نمی‌گیرم و دستانت را بگذار
یا حداقل مورب جهان، مماس کنم
خویشتن‌های بسیار نسل‌کُش شده‌اند و
معجزه‌ها را دور زده‌اند
دهانی پر خون به جا بگذار
قطراتش را در جام خویش نگهدار و بگریز
مرزبانی تو را به عقد در آورده ...

# Seyed Morteza Hamidzadeh

# Exile Me

Seyed Morteza Hamidzadeh

# Blood Offerings

پیشکش خون

## Exile Me

The one you see,

Is nobody

The one who

Sneers at us…


The habitual wrath

The agony of teeth ground from;

Insects that eat

Headscarf on head

The thought of the pit troubles


The number is on him

The offering of six bodies

And deriving solace on one's own place

We bend over him tranquilly

He is at the same place

## Seyed Morteza Hamidzadeh

He pinches your back softly

And with the return of your head

The final blow is blown on you!!!

او که می‌بینی ،
کسی نیست
او که بر ما
نیشخند می‌زند ...

**قهر همیشگی**
شیونِ دندان‌های به‌هم‌خورده از ؛
حشره‌هایی که به سر
روسری می‌خورند
فکر چاه‌ها عذاب می‌دهد

مَر به اوست
تقدیم شش تن
و آرام گرفتن بر جای خویش
آرام بر او خم می‌شویم
او همانجاست
آرام بر پشت‌ات نیشگون می‌گیرد
و با برگشتن سرت
ضربه نهایی، بر تو وارد می‌شود !!!

## Seyed Morteza Hamidzadeh

# Exile Me

Seyed Morteza Hamidzadeh

# Life Measured

مقیاس زندگی

# Exile Me

In sizes: small, normal, large

You reach the bloods with all your being

The hospital which

Amputates your limbs, removes your teeth

Its building-material on your head, desolate…


In the corner

Ammunition leads to crying

A body is felt

Get away from the neighbours and

Coldness

Surrounds the body…


The girl who is holding flowers

Thought of going to America

Thought of freethinking.

Vis-a-vis

Hospital in ruins

Screams...

## Exile Me

در سایز کوچک، نرمال، بزرگ
تمام قد به خون‌ها می‌رسی
بیمارستانی که
پایت را قطع، دندانت را جدا می‌کند
مصالحش را بر سرت ویران ...

در کُنج
مسلّحی گریه راه انداخته
پیکری، لمس می‌شود
بر انکاردها
دورتر از همسایگان می‌شوند و
سردی
بر جسمی احاطه ...

دخترکی گل به دست گرفته
فکر رفتن به آمریکا
فکر اندیشه‌هایی آزاد.
روبرو
بیمارستانی مخروبه
جیغ می‌زند ...

## Seyed Morteza Hamidzadeh

Seyed Morteza Hamidzadeh

# Consumed, Impartial
تلف شده در انصاف

# Exile Me

He goes, leaves me from

Impassionate hands

A mention of stray functions

Wine is flowing from everywhere…

I shall help you

See what sleeps and sings,

Dispatched pigeons and

I pass them on uncounted

Hands always on a heart that I don't have and

Myself from self

Your repenters, I count

A single turned into two and the collective

He chooses a scheme and

Discards the other males!

رود می‌گذرد از من از

دستانِ بی‌شهوت

توابینِ سرگردان ذکری که مرا

می از همه جاری است ...

به تو کمک خواهیم کرد

آنکه می‌بیند، می‌خوابد و می‌خواند

کبوترانِ ارسال و

از خود بی‌شمرده رد می‌کنم

دست‌های همیشه در قلبی که ندارم و

خود از خویش

توبه‌شدگان‌ات، می‌شمارم

جفت‌شده‌ی فردی و جمعی را

حیله راه می‌جوید و

باقی نرها را قِی می‌کند !

# Exile Me

# We Might Be Dead

مگر مرده باشیم

## Seyed Morteza Hamidzadeh

I didn't see you in world capitals

Let me pass

Through the embassy of bombings

I get hung

To the times when pianos shall play in restaurants and

Reduce distances to minimum…

We might be dead and

so I get close to you

The door of the chandelier of the circuital iron dome

Feels inferior to the city connected to you

When the fliers assembled on top of each other

I lose myself to the swarm

Inexistent connection of your being…

## Exile Me

در پایتختِ کشورها ندیدمت

بگذار گذر کنم

از سفارتِ بمباران‌ها

آویخته شوم

به دورانی که پیانوها در رستورانی بنوازند و

فاصله‌ای را به حداقل برسانند ...

مگر مرده باشیم و

اینقدر نزدیک‌ات شوم

در چلچراغی که گنبد آهنینِ مدارها

کم می‌آورد از شهری به تو وصل شده

وقتی پرونده‌ها روی هم جمع شدند

گم می‌کنم از ازدحام خویش

پیوندِ نبودِ هستی‌ات را ...

## Seyed Morteza Hamidzadeh

# Exile Me

Seyed Morteza Hamidzadeh

# Call Of The Disrupt
فریاد از هم گسیخته شدن

## Exile Me

You open the room's door

Sound of cries of the newborn take over

The twain shut in the room

Tumble from the coldness outside

Over the ruins of the ceiling that

Has reached its pinnacle

Sound of cries of a race

A race from the teeth that do not have your tolerance

And break from pressure of the root

Relax and turn the room into a voice

Music sends you kisses and

Extracts your ears from behind closed doors.

اتاق را باز می‌کنی

صدای گریه نوزاده‌ای فراگرفته

زوجی را که بسته در اتاقی

از سرمای بیرون می‌غلتند

بر ویرانه‌های سقفی که

اوج گرفته

صدای گریه قومی

قومی از دندان‌هایی که بر هم تابِ تو را ندارند

و می‌شکنند از فشارِ خاستگاه

آرام گیر و اتاقت را حنجره کن

موسیقی بر تو بوسه می‌فرستند و

گوش‌هایت را از درهای بسته خروج می‌کند.

# Not Duplicated, Transcended

تکرار نیست اما فراتر

## Seyed Morteza Hamidzadeh

Me replicas,

We are stubborn

When they search for television networks

Skeptic subtitles dominate

Your being has found meaning in it

Continuous demolition

In continuous roles

On the sides of lost lives

I reached myself, ready

And we passed through you

By you, without any moment

We sleep and find solace.

## Exile Me

منِ مدل‌ها

خیره‌ایم

وقتی به جستجوی شبکه‌های تلویزیونی بروند

زیرنویسِ شکاکان، چیره می‌شود

بر آن معنایافته در وجودت

انهدامِ همآره

در نقش‌های پیوسته

بر کناره‌هایی از جان‌های از بین رفته

آماده به خویش رسیدیم

و از میانات عبور کردیم

بی‌هیچ لحظه‌ای که در کنارت

به خواب رویم و آرام یابیم .

Seyed Morteza Hamidzadeh

# The End

پایان

# The Author

Seyed Morteza Hamidzadeh is a Persian poet who was born on August 31$^{st}$, 1991 in Masshad, Iran. His poetry can be found in magazines all around the world such as the WAF Anthology, eFiction, Zouch, Vivimus, Five Poetry, Maudlin House, and the Literati Quarterly. He is currently spending his days training in a military camp so that he may better defend against militants and extremists.

## Exile Me

www.ingramcontent.com/pod-product-compliance
Lightning Source LLC
Chambersburg PA
CBHW032037290426
44110CB00012B/840